WHEN I REACH FOR YOUR PULSE

WHEN I REACH FOR YOUR PULSE

RUSHI VYAS

FOUR WAY BOOKS
TRIBECA

Library of Congress Cataloging-in-Publication Data

Names: Vyas, Rushi, author.
Title: When I reach for your pulse / Rushi Vyas.
Description: New York : Four Way Books, [2023]
Identifiers: LCCN 2022033098 (print) | LCCN 2022033099 (ebook) |
ISBN 9781954245549 (paperback) | ISBN 9781954245556 (epub)
Subjects: LCGFT: Poetry.
Classification: LCC PS3622.Y37 W48 2023 (print) | LCC PS3622.Y37 (ebook)
| DDC 811/.6--dc23/eng/20220715
LC record available at https://lccn.loc.gov/2022033098
LC ebook record available at https://lccn.loc.gov/2022033099

This book is manufactured in the United States of America and printed on
acid-free paper.

Four Way Books is a not-for-profit literary press. We are grateful for the assistance
we receive from individual donors, public arts agencies, and private foundations
including the NEA, NEA Cares, the Literary Arts Emergency Fund, and the
New York State Council on the Arts, a state agency.

We are a proud member of the Community of Literary Magazines and Presses.

Contents

ॐ नमो नारायणाय

ॐ नमो नारायणाय

Notes

Effigy

I waited all my life for my father
to die and when he finally did I heard
the whip of voices caged within
his skull. In the neighborhood, maple
branches sprawled into each other, each
trunk an asthmatic wheeze summiting
the snake line, each limb heaving
into the next. A pattern ripples through
the absence of whom we scatter. I heard
my own pulse shelled by inheritance, felt
the stubborn flesh of a neck that snapped
its own beat. Outside, when people celebrate
the terrorist's death in the streets, I do not
leave my house. When my father finally
died, we cut him from the ceiling, fed him
sweets, dipped him in oil, and burned,
like an effigy, the voiceless body

Midwest Physics: First Law

Labor Day weekend, American drones whir
        over Syria, Somalia, Yemen, and Afghanistan, and
a father drives his son past acres of wheat
        up US 23, from suburban Ohio to Michigan Stadium.

They watch people run and hit. They eat overpriced
        pizza, dry cheese sliding off tomato sauce. They praise
the pregame F-16 flyover. Tailbone scratching metal,

        the child looks up: a striped flag spangled white
as the father's sweating forehead. The father clutches
        the boy's anxious hand in his, head bobbing

to the field and says, *All my hard work is for you, Bachu,*
        for this. No rushing the clock, they revel in pass
after incomplete pass. On third down, the boy stands to cheer,
        alone as the father sits, immovable.

Entomology // Mirage

I find you in the basement / suspended / pulse

       bare / though I keep reaching / for your carotid
       your neck / the cold throat / I roll

outside / away from your corpse / numb to the scald

       as Labor Day suns the black drive / I walk backward
       two days in time / into the park / mindless where I stumble

near a cicada / kicking / stuck / dying

       lift its shell from the puddle / try / to warm it /
       in palm / I do / *all I could* / but / *all I could*

fears the spine / the crunch / the nail

       between fingertip and neck / the unflinching / thin
       exoskeleton between rage / and vulnerability

I gave my entomologist friend / your body

       to hang behind glass / mounted on her wall / there
       below the jugular / a rope / tied to my larynx

I do / *all I could* / to drag through tar

      and haze to your funeral to discover / *enough* /
      if this rope will slacken / or choke

or break

Funeral: Durga Puja

red hibiscus petals represent names   names signifying things forgotten
the same can be said for each finger flick of water onto the body   this drop
lands on the sandalwood border—   a ring   the sun's outer rim limning
the body's ten arms   each arm wielding sweets and blades   this is how
destruction begins with sugar   right hand spoons water   waters body
repeat   the idol is mother deified on a flowerbed   offer grains of rice
each grain a representation of the forgotten   offer milk and rice and water
until the body cannot differentiate itself from nourishment   hide the idol's
lion feet in petals   flowers bleed onto the leopard rug and silken legs of
the worshipper   in this manner lines blur between finger and hand and
organism and room   in this manner   truth reveals its fire mouth and the
self is scorched by the divo   namastasyai namastasyai namastasyai namoh
namah

                    bow to her   bow to
                    her   bow to her   nature is
                    everywhere the same

Beads

We find a letter in the house from St. V's, a summons
to a meeting to discuss suspension of the two
letters following your name, the memo dated

two days before today, the day I find
your emptied shell strung up
by a thick, silver—
                                    Your employees tell us
about the clack of rudraksha beads you slapped,
hand in pocket. You took a patient's phone,

checked for spyware. You left probes in bodies,
exited exam rooms to mutter in your office, beads
clacking. Against your clamor,
                                    I lift my palm
superstitious to the chest to beads that hang
from my neck. *Bapu*, I say, and will to see you standing

where the imprints of your feet remain in the living
room carpet, palms together in front of Ganesh, Shiva, Mataji,
Dadaji, Krishna, and Saraswati, standing in the posture of

prayer, every day, three times a day, never reverie-
orbed, shut-eyed like Mom singing bhajans.
I finger the beads around my carotid, let

rough-edged tree seeds massage
fingertips. They say, *Sorry*. My mantra replies,
It's not your fault   It's not your fault   It's not—

Suicide Note in absentia, *Part 1*

Another night in an empty house. All quiet,
but the knocking brain. Back tight, I lie on the cold foyer's peach
marble floor. I worked so hard for years for insurance against the
noise of silence. Now you are gone, my *wife;—* You've left me
in order to build a place of your own. The open envelope from
the hospital sits by the stove's dead coils: my sweats, curled in a
hamper, unclean. No agarbatti burning . . . no kids I can reach . . .
only their portraits framed beneath the chandelier. Another night
in an empty home;—

~

—"*Gulu Bhai!*" Moti Mummy howls from her
demented room. I heed the call that occupies me. "You must occupy
the mind against dreams." She governed the Bhavnagar Estate with
a broomstick, left servants to sweep on knees with rags. She said,
"Be a surgeon greater than your father." She locked me in a room
upstairs with books. Delivered meals. Smacked my spine with the
broomstick each time my eyes wandered from textbook to the kayri
and tamarind trees through the window. She occupied my mind:
her Brahmin whip. Now, hear her wail at 3am, in Ohio, in the

white, modern home I built her. She shouts, again, her name for me: "Gulu Bhai!" Pink boy;— I am slapped by the hand that made me.

~

—Under the foyer's chandelier, I hurt from love because love is what I do I love you and you forget. When we moved to Detroit, I worked until I fell asleep in the hospital cot beside vending machines so you'd never have to work again. Those white doctors, my peers, abused me because they could because they knew I would work and work. 40-hour shifts under fluorescence. All for you, I worked. And now, you're gone;— Mistake to let you raise our betās: they, too, learned ingratitude. Their portraits in the foyer hollow as a white physician's pledge to recommend me. You must ablate, like cells, memories too rapidly multiplying. ~~They have not;~~ — ~~They will not;~~ — *They* MUST—*bring you back.*

Attachment

Statements and bills obstruct breath.
Amidst the paper mass left by the husband
my mother tried to leave, the arteries in her eyes
sprawl. We fall to the floor around a lit candle,
its scent kin to the pine freshner
that once swayed from the rearview mirror
of her forest green Plymouth Voyager
driven to karate to violin to anything
the American University might reward.

~

The mother allows the eight-year-old boy to sit shotgun for the first time   He watches red cars glint in the sun as they drive home from karate class   She tells him he needs to learn his slokas   She's making him sing at Temple Sunday where incense smoke soaks into his clothes   The boy wishes shotgun did not come with a price

~

Any neighbor's sideways glance or *Dateline*
episode unfurled my father's paranoia. We lived
on lock and dial up. To escape, eleven-year-old I
called a chatroom stranger. Bapu found the phone
bill I'd stashed at the bottom of a kitchen drawer
and summoned Mom into the master bedroom.
Her emergence revealed the bruises she'd worked
to hide, unlocked the songs she'd stowed alive.

~

Her voice distracts the eight-year-old boy from the *whoosh* of shiny
cars passing by but he knows better than to bargain with a voice that
stills him   *Yaakundendu tushaarahaara dhavalaa*   she sings & he
repeats sullenly   He repeats as she corrects his *duhs* & *dhuhs*   Her
voice soothes but he remembers the lady in *Apollo 13* humming her
sweet song in the shower before her wedding ring falls to the drain
Bad omen his mother explained   Beauty will not lull him into false
security   That mother's voice could drift out of his reach at any
moment   This is why they teach detachment at Temple

~

In the living room, I learned to discern
a father's mood from flickers:
widened eye, force of a stride,
pursed call of Mom's name
quavering down the hall. I learned
every closed door wields a blade of light below—
how to press my cheek still against it, listen.

~

The boy stays sullen as he repeats   *Yaakundendu tushaarahaara*
dhavalaa   He feigns apathy   *Saraswati bhagava—*   She
interrupts   *bhuh* not *buh*   He repeats   *Saraswati bhagavati*

~

Each time she returned from the den
and my gaze asked if there was abuse,
she shook her head before the gods
in our living room.
                    Oblique,
the transmission of knowledge.
Her labor: to shape our ears into spades,
sow parables for a silenced mouth.

~

The boy repeats in his head until the syllables that are not yet
words loop   until the sounds that are not yet symbols are recited
automatically when she wakes him from the couch to go sleep upstairs
The song—   *Yaaveena varadandamandi takaraa*   creates a sail—
Yashvesta padmaasanaa   of syllables to clutch   if only in the dark

Morning Chant: Cave

Gurumūrtim smarennityam
Gurunāma sadā japet,

follow the command
of she / who issues no commands
who offers a hand / only if asked /
facilitation is

simple / pick up the phone
I do not / I do not
answer / cold scapula
in the cavern of his now /
his last reverb / the last
I will hear his voice /
stalactite in the voicemail's
hollow / *please call me back* /
without apology without appellating
Bachu / tone cloaking
need / I do not heed
watered rock's spear / dance
under his tie / at a friend's wedding
forget our earlier drive / he only
a passenger / grip stealing

the steering wheel / pulling us
onto the curb / he arrived
at the door with a heap
of dry cleaning / they say
that's a sign I should have
recognized / instead I / tied his tie
around my neck / his tie he tied
so many times / I'd phoned
so often thinking *change* /
now abrogate / think
lesson / loosen my collar
kick / shimmy / in a cave
of my own construction

follow the command
of / who holds the vitreous
flakes of my eyes / together
by diaphanous thread

Gurorājñām prakurvīta,
Guror-anyanna bhāvayet.

Conditional Bridges

My sister's voice is a shotgun
fired and reloaded. We drive up US 23
past the border, the breeding deer, the farmed

miles, the hunting store. Her cries mime
the stilted flap of wild turkeys
from earth to highway pines, where they rest

wind-beaten wings. My ears are conditional
bridges: the infrastructure for breath's heft. *Heavy,*
cousin Nikhil called the death inscribed now

in her lungs. She will not sleep for months.
Each dorm door slammed or hinge squeaking
open into night—a bell of her Bapu leaving

footsteps down the vacant hall: moonlit branches
slicing windows: the geometries of flight:
birds too feathered to fly. She cannot escape

the propulsive fire of mourning. Under the spell
of her roommate's lungs, my sister traces light
and shadow arched on the wall: death postponed

by the chest's rise and fall. *All that falls is caught.*
Unless it doesn't stop, like her larynx bewildered
by the air death pulls from the living. Eyelids flit

above any throat stranded in the rip
of the rhetorical *Why?* All I can do is sit
awash in all I cannot bring myself to say.

Viveka Vairāgya at the Amtrak Station

One train slumbers. Dust
scatters on tracks. The 7pm
to Chicago strums away. A woman

waves, rubs with right shoulder
the bone under her eye. Under
a tree, a lark refuses sleep, preens

sunset's blade's burnt strobe. A bottle
shattered rusts. Kick it aside, watch—
fly-pocked apple core, damp

cement in sun. The platform leaves
more what than whom. Grief
walks me where I will not board.

Double Slit

On the tongue, dim hovering
over basement cement, light scatters
grey through the transom above
my dead father. Stiff as sugarcane,
I stand. Golden beams fleck grains
of dust into his mouth. Light molds
an ejected tongue into a tumor:
my metastatic tremble: *No.*

Think of light: my body approaching—
now wave; his hanging—now particle.
When I reach for his pulse
I collapse. Behind the door's double slit
the suspended body dies when seen.
Perhaps if I look away—   *No.*

Two days earlier, in sunlight,
in the car, Bapu closer to my throat
than his mind. One moment shaking,
cursing his *goddamned* son. The next,
still apology, open palm caressing
his *Bachu's* flat head. The visible
spectrum flutters in rearview.   *No.*

Blink: phantasm; flicker: shadow; quiver:
basement furnace burning behind the neck,
thieving his body to warm our home. I offer
prasad to the murti of his mangled tongue,
pour milk past hungry mouths into the gutter.
Across the globe, a monk leaps from a mountain
to return as rain. The prayer's scaffold falls.

When I Reach for Your Pulse

I

I am trying to get to the matter in matter that is the [   ] in matter

the [   ] that is fluid—   melted candlewax   new moon

Aum   Lake Erie—   the terrain personalities and air

that possess [   ]   the wind is a muted vowel in the brush of pine

branches and sidewalk leaves whose aspirated breaths roll

into   up   and into the human ear

2

when I reach for your pulse I think I hear my name   I hear traffic squeaking on

tar   in milliseconds between inhaled sound and exhaled memory   soundwaves

shake the ear's mridangam's cells made of [   ] and Rutherfordian atoms—

ninety-nine percent [   ] tiny bones marrow-filled—

ninety-nine percent [   ] muted rage my heirloom [   ]   *Thoom!*

passes vibration through the snail to neurons chanting—   *name   name   name*—

rattling the Rutherfordian brain   which escapes into [   ] into background

traffic   transmutes [   ] to fear   a gulp

3

rising [   ] means to make itself heard   somewhere on the spectrum

color longs to elongate its wavelength constraint   what white friends call tanning

I call repression   when I reach for your [   ] I see mountains   hear

no laughter streaming to the Atlantic   ritual blue deepening to a fraught

cerulean where rules lean and middle wavelengths reflect water   jal

also ninety-nine percent [   ] gifted body by the spasmodic waltz

of electrons   breathe in oxygen and hydrogen [   ] displaced from another

breathe out carbon [   ] render it lifeless   in (Brahma)   out (Shiva)

along the street   walk brick by brick over ants   smile   try not

4

to think of the cicada's dying hum   I assert imaginings as musts

let my mind be the [   ] be the water comprising 70% of your body where

no thought lingers   let me run toward the longest wavelengths in your neck

strengthen lungs   expand thoracic [   ] to protect the Kingfisher

displaced behind your ribs   theory says if I repeat this touch infinitely

my fingertips eventually will flap like ghosts through skin   let me retreat

into the [   ] beneath the banyan root's crook where I rest when I sit

closing my eyes   where I pull air through my nose

5

in the subconscious tense   when I reach for your pulse I speak to myself

in imperatives   hold this matter in your palm   feel [   ] knock

your fist   the half-moon lights the the eight-year-old child in you   run

to spin the precarious Rosenthal cube pivoted in cement   slow steps

churning legs   spinning [   ] the block's electrons shift perpetual

perpetuate illusion   the body does not crumble for unexpected reason

all matter fluxes   danger without escape   watch the cube

spin like his car endlessly around a cul-de-sac   inescapable who slowed

only by way of skin of hands of wrists of arms of joints of nails   all magic

starts in the vast [   ] between electrons in fingertips—

wands attempting a final converse: If you appear then you must disappear

If you disappear then you must—

ॐ नमो नारायणाय

ॐ नमो नारायणाय

ॐ नमो नारायणाय

ॐ नमो नारायणाय

ॐ नमो नारायणाय

ॐ नमो नारायणाय

ॐ नमो नारायणाय

ॐ नमो नारायणाय

ॐ नमो नारायणाय

ॐ नमो नारायणाय

ॐ नमो नारायणाय

ॐ नमो नारायणाय

ॐ नमो नारायणाय

ॐ नमो नारायणाय

ॐ नमो नारायणाय

ॐ नमो नारायणाय

ॐ नमो नारायणाय

ॐ नमो नारायणाय

ॐ नमो नारायणाय

ॐ नमो नारायणाय

ॐ नमो नारायणाय

ॐ नमो नारायणाय

ॐ नमो नारायणाय

Love Story with Rolex

> *But, I also think that epigenetic trauma can produce keloids—the ugly*
> *thing that overreacts to environmental stress . . . I think it makes us*
> *worriers, not warriors—compulsive performers of what Vijay Prashad*
> *has called "the inward turn" among many South Asians in the US who*
> *prefer the accumulation of securities over the exercise of their rights.*
> *—Divya Victor*

The man who earned the money Mom used to raise me
owned a gold Rolex. He wore it every day. At night, turning

in, he placed it in the corner of the closet drawer with his wallet, checks,
socks, patient notes, and handkerchiefs. He would not wear the watch

when, rotli between thumb and forefingers, he scooped shāk
and dāl with bhāt. He wore the watch with crisp white shirts,

glossy ties, and custom fit Mephistos. He wore the watch with blue jeans
and polos at Don Pablo's. The Rolex, he thought, earned the respect

of Catholics and Jews, potential patients, clients, investment
experts, and important administrators. The man who earned

the money Mom used to raise me drove recklessly against
his risk aversion. I would cling to the locked Acura door handle

around each corner. Rolex lived for these moments—
quickened wrist blood beating against its cold ribs. The man

who earned the money Mom used to raise me kept Rolex polished,
listened to its needs. When its ticking slowed, he promptly consulted

its mechanic. He knew how to love it and had it been
left to my authority I would have let the watch burn with him

when he left this world. The man who earned
the money Mom used to raise me never asked

Rolex what kept it ticking all night, alone in its drawer, and
why would he? It was a watch. The watch had little to tell.

Proverb *in absentia*

a bird in hand is worth
squeezing the life out of

a body mostly nothing
cloaked in rib & feather

a tie ornamented with wings
pivots around your trachea

air & bone lined with skin
stubble grown waiting

too long for the two in the bush
grave mistake you say

to keep palms empty
like the atoms that mold

hands out of negative charges
groan for form they cannot hold

desire violent to bond

Midwest Physics: Second Law

Every lie begets another: a proverb
you would have preached. Were it a penny
saved . . . Were we earlier to rise . . .

I never told you about the woman
I lived with in Michigan. Or the cat. You never
knew, with the money you gave me I drank.

When Mom left you she moved
onto my couch and I told you
I didn't know her whereabouts.

When the British came to India
they studied the habits of the Rajas,
pitted kings against each other.

Without weapons I studied
your routine. Midday doze. Snore
on the sofa to Peter Jennings. Hours long

nap after work before 10pm dāl, bhāt,
shāk, rotli. I learned to press your calves
before you rose. Understood your temper

as one to fear and tend. I'd rush
to grab the *Toledo Blade* from the driveway and
make a playful show of stealing the Sports page.

All those momentary, imagined reprieves . . .
I did not know how to speak
an honest word to my father.

Bapu, where is Mom's family?
Explain the black under her eye.
You taught me each lie could buy a night.

Making Ghee in This American Kitchen

The refrigerator is dying

The museless voice calls

Ecology our butter bell

Smother fire

Clarify another pound

Clear the kitchen counter

Of all serrated blades

Hypocrisy is hope

Conflate heat source and burned

Pages the sheets ablute

Unlaundered fathers

Say only the name

Of this country of unapology

In this country of unapology

Nāranga aurantium

in memory of Srinivas Kuchibhotla
after the patient who told my mother to "go back where she came from"

the orange seed
does not   disappear

or appear just
regenerates   in the grove

its crenulated face   greens
through mid-November   oval

winter   in a city   in Kansas in a city
in Ohio in ambiguous cities in ambiguous states

teeth pierce a stranger's skin   acid gushes
onto the sidewalk   under satellite-marred

skies   another dead   chin drips
sinensis   our grove reaps the bark we've sown

Remembrance

your dad saved my life three times
the man speaks of a man

you never fully knew   picture a cape
on stiff shoulders raised   understand

never for the first time: exhaust
leaving his silver car each morning

mother's harmonium pulled to closure

the speaking man's cheeks purple
his jaw finds your clavicle   you're jealous

of his tears   his hued huff   he squeezes
your back too hard   says *he was a great man*

try to comprehend him: rusted undercarriage
soft rock daily on his commute   you mutter

thank you   you repeat   *thank you*

I Saw You and I Learned This, Beloved

grieve not the scriptures say   Sage Kapila
        defines death   *the return of cause*

                          Tujhe dekha to yeh jaana sanam

I bow as the customer passes their finished dish
        to my hands   read my palm's lifeline

it says *you'll live heavy and long*
        before tracing your cause   all I hold

                          Pyara hota hai deewana sanam

crumbs   flayed remains
        chunk of naan I sneak to my mouth

before the plate ends in a bus tub   don't we all
        bathe in demise like a fetish   smiling

                          Ab yahan se kahan jaaye hum

at his funeral   namaskaaring
        respect   stroking the nails

that tied his neck to its cause

    I scrub chili grime to Hindi songs his timbre—

                Teri baahon mein mar jaaye hum

elbow shudders against a plate stack

    white porcelain discs spinning

exoticized jasmine in barren fields

    petals in puja before shatter   I reach

for the broom   smile for reason

    these crooked lips   his frayed remainder

                Tujhe dekha to yeh jaana sanam

sweeping the scattered I

    squint for any glint in the shards

Raga of Bapu's Hand as Brueghel's *Icarus* with Rilke and a Swami in It

now he is opening the box   the boy
opening   the father above looking on
hair combed and flowing like blackened leaves

of a willow   arching above the scalp while the boy hides
behind the lid as though it's a simile   as though the boy
does not know what lies in the box   which he hopes

might carry more than the letters of a fading
booklet   one with an ochre-robed brahmin man on the cover
and its title   *Thoughts of Power*

      the father's hand swings up and lands
gently on the boy's hair   strokes
side to side the black like a pond ebbs

after catching a body that flew too close
to the sun   the father is a gulu sky
after monsoons   unknowable   the father

in affection   holds shoulders
like an undetermined tense   like a boy
too young for fluency in the body

language of one brow here another
below the bridge   where snow stifles
the certain world

       the boy closes
the box   he looks to the man through
eyes white with the season of unknowing

trying to remember what he will
pretend to forget—   an open palm
caressing his hair like the shruti note of rain

blown diagonal by northwest wind   hammering
the corner of a roof and streaming down to collect
like a child   into whoever's arms will welcome its return

Suicide Note in absentia, *Part 2*

—*Our families introduced us, Gujarati Brahmins together by the stars' will. At dinner with family, we nodded, consulted the astrologer, and then married in a new country, in Cerritos, your sister's backyard, a grass sliver encased in brick. Our small ceremony . . . No alcohol, no pomp, few friends . . . Just the Pandit, the family, the havan. Flower petals and rice into the fire. I tightened our knot with each step. No need for words. Your tears under sun knew the meaning of Pandit Ji's slokas, the surrender of your lower family for mine. Then, we were living together, flown for good from India's dust, to Cincinnati for my training and your chemistry PhD, a degree I deemed disposable;— You must keep occupied the mind.*

~

—*On the fourth night of July, you were in labor. At Toledo Hospital, I scrubbed in for no surgery. Your hair frayed on the cot arriving to term after three failed pregnancies. We'd been waiting for him. In the morning, I watched late Wimbledon breakfast, the Swede Edberg defeating Becker on the corner TV. Though I knew the boy was mine, I questioned you (the broomstick's serve and snap);— If the boy had not arrived, I feared you'd leave*

43

me;— Your defiance had been rising. When I threatened to kick you out of my house, you said, "Tell me when, and I'll go." I knew to obey my inheritance;— Nothing would be given or forgiven;— You must TAKE what you want from this world.

~

—The first day of September and we waited in the hospital again. It was your birthday, soon to be shared with a daughter. Our son, five, accompanied me on my rounds, his crooked smile greeting nurses . . . Not long ago, he fit unconscious in my lap and we'd fall asleep on the sofa watching the Tigers into the ninth each summer night, my hand caressing the flat back of his head. Now, a sister, he thought we would buy from the store. The voices quiet . . . In those moments, I forgot you and the wealth;— How easily it all could slip beyond my grasp.

ॐ नमो नारायणाय

ॐ नमो नारायणाय

ॐ नमो नारायणाय

ॐ नमो नारायणाय

ॐ नमो नारायणाय

ॐ नमो नारायणाय

ॐ नमो नारायणाय

ॐ नमो नारायणाय

ॐ नमो नारायणाय

ॐ नमो नारायणाय

ॐ नमो नारायणाय

ॐ नमो नारायणाय

ॐ नमो नारायणाय

ॐ नमो नारायणाय

ॐ नमो नारायणाय

ॐ नमो नारायणाय

ॐ नमो नारायणाय

ॐ नमो नारायणाय

ॐ नमो नारायणाय

ॐ नमो नारायणाय

ॐ नमो नारायणाय

ॐ नमो नारायणाय

ॐ नमो नारायणाय

ॐ नमो नारायणाय

scaf • fold (n)

1. A temporary platform, either supported from below or suspended from above, on which workers sit or stand when performing tasks at heights above the ground.
2. [. . .]
3. A platform used in the execution of condemned prisoners, as by hanging or beheading.

—The American Heritage Dictionary

The scaffold is a pause, an inflection of passage. It accommodates us in a shivering.

—Lisa Robertson

Scaffold

do not make beautiful the noose   or its pedestal
the scaffold is almost a catastrophe

        my love studies the score   their role as Mother Marie
        in Poulenc's *Dialogues des Carmélites*   T disagrees
        with the portrayal of the historical Marie as a villain
        pleading for her Carmelite Sisters' martyrdom   yet
        ultimately denied her willful death   the order's lonely survivor

(von le Fort)

        During the French Terror, *Marie de l'Incarnation believed that her*
        Sisters would mount the scaffold singing . . . She sensed that their
        singing *effaced all sense of time, it effaced space and the bloody Place de*
        la Révolution.

one year after my father died
T's arias stilled the hostel corridor
my thoughts dispersed into the incessant
horns of Mysore streets

ten days after Bapu died   I returned

meditated on the concrete above which he hung

there   in dim light   I heard

the mob of voices that escaped his skull

Never would I have thought that such a song could leave the lips of those condemned to death. I had been deeply disturbed. But when I heard this singing I grew quiet. Creator spiritus, Creator spiritus, I seemed to hear these two words again and again. They cast anchor within me. (von le Fort)

Creator spiritus   Creator spiritus

Om namo nārāyanāya   Om namo nārāyanāya

~

(Robertson) *The history of scaffolding has been dismantled. We can't write this history because there are so few documents—only a slim sheaf of photographs. So we study the construction of the present and form theories.*

my love disputes the male
librettist's retelling of Marie

T imbues the character with resolution
not stubbornness   resistance in the service

of something beyond blood

Portrait of Bapu and Son as Investment Account Tied Up in Probate
If you are packaged in a bundle   I will not notice
the oil spill you fund   the murder of Sioux people you
bankroll   The great flag of commerce will shield
me from sun
                    But I am the dog
with no owner to blanket my ears during fireworks
On the fourth all I hear is grenade   gunshot   bomb

                    I walk through Denver   rest under the city's cranes
                    wood and steel reflections   built to consume gaze while

                    every sixteen minutes a person cuts their own breath
                    each suicide   an execution into which guilt shivers

Life should not be shattered by machinery. And yet, this is the very symbol of our destiny. . . . the guillotine is not responsible, it shudders at nothing, it destroys indifferently everything that is brought to it, the noble and the pure as well as the most criminal. . . . Perhaps it is the very crown of chaos, a crown worn by the enthusiasm of the soulless mob . . .

(von le Fort)

had I placed the bell of your stethoscope   on your skull
had I listened to the Gujarati Hindi and English voices between

your clamorous poles   affection to conniption   man who stood
three times a day before Bhagavan   who headbutted his wife and later

his son   would my hearing have appeased your mob?

       "He always smiled   I always thought
       your dad was so kind   So happy"

Creator spiritus   Creator spiritus

~

(Robertson) *When the baby is born there is no place to put it . . . . A temporary scaffolding is set up for it, an altar to ephemerality . . . . so long as he can go on pretending that it is permanent he is happy.*

M says   "The Uncles in our community are helpless"
in your last months   all you could say: "You *must* get her back"

         despair for an Uncle: when he must occupy the kitchen
         relearn how to use the skillet   load the dishwasher
         and sleep alone under the appliance hum

A scaffold sketches a body letting go of proprietary expectation, or habit, in order to be questioned by change. It is architecture's unconscious displayed as a temporary lacework: a garden in other words . . . *(Robertson)*

(Kan) *Origin of garden: Middle English gardin, from Anglo-French gardin,*
jardin, of Germanic origin; akin to Old High German gart—an
enclosure. The words yard, court and Latin hortus all refer to an
enclosed space. Love has to be kept away from the world.

when Foi and my cousins visited from Rajkot   Bapu called me
into the den   closed the door and instructed   "Don't let them
get close   They must not be trusted"

Mother Marie feared that the young Carmelite Sister Blanche harbored *(von le Fort)*
doubt, that this doubt left her ill-prepared for martyrdom. Marie said,
"Do you really wish to appear before the Saviour with this mortal fear in your
heart?" Blanche replied, *"Reverend Mother, I do not wish to be disloyal."*

after weeks attempting to console her American brother
Foi returned to Rajkot abruptly   had she perceived
a threat?   what pasts congeal in the throat?
Foi will not speak   no Uncle or Auntie goes on record
loyalty protects the brahmin man

~

(Robertson) *Scaffolding is analogy. It explains what a wall is without being a wall. Perhaps it describes by desiring the wall.*

we build scaffolds of names to buttress the self
my planks: Son Partner Brother Son-in-Law Poet Educator Indian American
your planks: MD Urologist Husband Father Gujarati American Brahmin Wealthy

after the Terror   did Marie—stripped of her Carmelite
order and denied the martyrdom of the guillotine—have any
remaining planks on which to construct herself?   Her history
novelized   has been dismantled

my love struggles to inhabit Marie
their desire for nuance conflicts
with the director's tropes
T refuses to detach and diminish
the Marie they've come to know

55

. . . the scaffold wants to fall away from support . . . . It finds its stabilities in the transitions between gestures. (Robertson)

When she learned that she would not be permitted to join her Sisters in martyrdom, Marie de l'Incarnation's *face first showed that peculiar expression in which one could suddenly see how she must have looked as a child.* (von le Fort)

in the space between curse   and apology—   your eyes
red rilles through morning mist   your skin a thawing sound

from the driver's seat   I remembered   you once were a boy
it was then and there   my mind bowed to *shoulds*

Creator spiritus   Creator spiritus
Om namo nārāyanāya   Om namo nārāyanāya

~

from the Denver street   clutch hands
watch cranes build walls they cannot enter

permit your city a stable   identity as though
you share no kinship with what holds you

at our last meeting I said   "Bapu   you need help"
he shook in reply   "No *You* need help"
I wish I had said   "Yes I *too* need help"
instead my last words   "I love you"

if I'd become a surgeon   I would slice precise
through the scalp   excise the tongues that strangle a family

Ah! my friend, do not think that these people were not capable of good impulses. The mob is always capable of good impulses! That is the very thing that makes a mob of people: that they are capable of anything at all! (von le Fort)

Om namo nārāyanāya   Om namo nārāyanāya
Creator spiritus   Creator spiritus

~

months into our relationship   T began rehearsing
for a role in *Dead Man Walking*
rehearsals raging at death row   occupied their mind

alongside our growing love   grief
fontanels of one skull

I imagine you living alone for months   a hoarder
chambered in scraped pots   your thoughts
fricative as late Coltrane's *Cosmos* squawks
before the drugs and brain demanded he rest

There is then a still, profound existence that remains, nameless and
unmanifest; it is neither light nor darkness.

I face what I project and cannot understand   your fear
of image—log kya kahenge?—of losing the load-bearing
plank of *M.D.*   under threat of collapse   your coatless
body could not withstand the mob   you lost
weight   lost patients   you died

we too want something that's neither inside nor outside   neither a space nor *(Robertson)*
a site   in an inhabitable surface that recognizes us   we'd like to gently sway
then we would be happy

(von le Fort) When Marie thought she would be sacrificed by execution to appease
the Lord, she could not hide her joy. Upon seeing Marie, Madame
Lidoine remarked, *"Why, you are aglow as an angel my daughter.*
What has happened to you?"

Creator spiritus   Creator spiritus
Om namo nārāyanāya   Om namo nārāyanāya

~

after the sheriff cut the tether

you fell   he helped me turn your body

onto its back   so you could face

the light   so I could face you

stroke your hair   press my ear

to the chest   of your body rendered evidence

I am still looking at you

in a light that will take years to arrive   *(Sharif)*

I *must* still look at you

Beneficiary

      Diploma stained with blood of Sioux and sea

      Brahmin son

      they will keep silent to protect you

      blame women for what you do

      O, suicide's son

      what will you relinquish?

Never would I have thought that such a song could leave the lips of those condemned to death . . . . The singing effaced all sense of time, it effaced space and the bloody Place de la Révolution. Creator spiritus, Creator spiritus . . . *cast anchor within me.*

And if the voices I hear are only grief's imagination . . .

unstable as origin   our bodies express as executioners
blend into something I cannot name   an asymptote
where guilt and culpability refuse abutment

my love is drained
after their last performance as Marie

T vows never to sing the role again

Creator spiritus   Creator spiritus

A scaffold sketches a body letting go . . . in order to be questioned by change.

the noose gifted your spine permission to unroll
I wish to have been present at your willful execution

ॐ नमो नारायणाय

ॐ नमो नारायणाय

ॐ नमो नारायणाय

ॐ नमो नारायणाय

ॐ नमो नारायणाय

ॐ नमो नारायणाय

ॐ नमो नारायणाय

ॐ नमो नारायणाय

ॐ नमो नारायणाय

ॐ नमो नारायणाय

ॐ नमो नारायणाय

ॐ नमो नारायणाय

ॐ नमो नारायणाय

ॐ नमो नारायणाय

ॐ नमो नारायणाय

ॐ नमो नारायणाय

ॐ नमो नारायणाय

ॐ नमो नारायणाय

ॐ नमो नारायणाय

ॐ नमो नारायणाय

ॐ नमो नारायणाय

ॐ नमो नारायणाय

ॐ नमो नारायणाय

Cremation :: Translation

"Cremator On" push
Om Namo Nārāyanāya
Mantra for our keeping
Om Namo Nārāyanāya
Spoon parting corpse lips
Om Namo Nārāyanāya
Condole the mortician
Om Namo Nārāyanāya

Gangājal :: water
Tulsi leaves :: spades
Jasmine :: fragrance mask
Six pinda :: ancestors
around the derigored body
Black sesame :: fists
Chandan :: sandalwood
Soul :: barefoot on cold floor
Kumkum :: turmeric and slaked lime
Embalmer's grey :: patience
Ghee :: fuel
Gangājal :: water

Om Namo Nārāyanāya
Refrain :: the mangled tongue

Om Namo Nārāyanāya

Hammer the nerve

Om Namo Nārāyanāya

"Cremator On" push

Om Namo Nārāyanāya

Flesh to fire

Om Namo Nārāyanāya

Gangājal :: water

Om Namo Nārāyanāya

Gangājal :: water

Diaspora

light sweeps through the warbler I find lying beside autumn's
rusted road   wing clipped   body hollow

I carry the bird to heal indoors under an inverted wire
garbage basket   a cage in a room where the beak sputters

reverb   the bird returns   into the breast
where electrons hum and mingle   making audible

the pause in a futile wing flap   revealing the silence
of a half-empty   half-material imagining self

searching for reminders perpetual
this hearing the ocean in passing traffic

Funeral: Pilgrimage

Cold water rests in a bucket on the grout-creased square-tile floor   A silver-green lizard suctions up and down the washroom wall   Yellow smog soaks through the screened window outside which the black dogs   who live under the bamboo scaffolding surrounding the perpetually under-construction cement building across the street   nuzzle the sides of their young   Fingers test water before pouring over greying hair to rouse eyelids   This is how to construct a self   lather rinse dry clothe fill with idli and clove-laced sambar nod in greeting and leave   breathe the air thrumming with Ring Road traffic   dust-pocked   tulsi-scented from the row of bushes flanking the gravel road and giving way   in moments when the wind is right   to the dead rodent stench of the lot turned neighborhood landfill one block away Walking through swamp air burning in rising day   feet crunch gravel past a windowless hospital   approach a pond whose far side's green field   lush with palm trees and tall grasses   collects neighborhood men's motions   A Kingfisher flaps and settles on bramble floating in the pond's center   It finds no gap for reflection

Move   move   move   Walking
through haze heals   One foot tramples
another's holy

Morning Chant: Scatter

Guruvaktra-sthitam brahma
prāpyate tatprasādatah,

That tongue tells all
I need to know   unties all I want
and what I want is not thought
not intuition not negation

Any cord can be a noose
Any cord can be the thread
I wear around my shoulder
an oppressor's pageantry   my
brahmin sash

In the ceremony   Pandit Ji
asks me to flip the sacred
from shoulder to shoulder
nine times   signifying something
lost in hours of solitary puja

At the Maumee River
I scatter dust with flowers
and rice   Eye whites stare
at brown banks   We chant
and smell memory's breath

68

turmeric in warm milk   Who knows
how to heal even when exiled
to be imagined   I hear my mother
in my head   four requests
Embrace   Let go   Stop   Act

The first contradicts Uncle's *Be a man*
no tears   though my eyes cannot let go
the mangled tongue   the tongue that taught
me about the Bad Boys   racist preached

no BMW's   slurped chai with Rodman's
flare   and breathy sung *Tujhe dekha*
to yeh jaana sanam   that dead organ

tethered to pipes in the ceiling
I cannot shake the mangled tongue
Image arrests like jasmine

scent in hair   try and wash it
away   try and wash and
fail   at last watch the remains

of tree and man float grey in brown
water   flanked by white
flowers   sweet petals sinking

with all these grains drying the river
Bapu's ash brushes onto the berm

I wonder how anyone arrives
to ocean without a thread

what I want is not a what
here at language's limits   it flickers
a tongue living

guror-dhyānam sadā kuryāt
kulastrī svapateryathā.

Exegesis as Quarter Cento from the Wagah Border

When the Beast emerges
from the western sea to haul
this gelatinous body   people
laugh   it will never pillar a house

I'm the only Dimwit in town   I've seen
me this unbuilt room: tongue inside
the mouth inside the throat inside a severing
cut eye   or a melancholy wordless moaning
through my hunger for air   asthmatic

What seas seize sees   we grind
lenses to an impossible   They will clink
as ice in your glass of rum   They were the exit
wounds   but of what then   or for what   is this voice
I hear?   This voice: an analytical eye on details
in the print: two shadows in the shadow color

Just ahead   *a torch*   I think   held there
This house as I see it is a sort of *airy*
Solace: words given up to arcades
of bright coronal loops   Laughter
is shattered articulation   Like kinematics

and mass and velocity   it's a small part
of the pantomime   I prefer stillness
People (you) are rectified of themselves
(yourselves)   You lap these worlds
into your burning mouths and swallow them

Postcard from Amritsar

bahēn   the world says you own nothing
your blood hasn't spilled to earn   anything

you bleed they'll reclaim   your bare brick-scratched arm
swings past the machine of city   of country   to survive

you leap into a dark well   echo
where bullet casings cannot follow   you carry

a solitary creek within   one that flows lit with sun
green ducks   plastic bags   dirty socks   scattered

leaves   one that babbles joyful nonsense
                                        I dreamed

last night   a river dammed with rust
when I woke   a raven wailed

outside my window   the wail outlasts
the dream   the stream survives its source

Ars Poetica

The coach wanted
me to run faster, like a husky,
and so tied me to his. My legs'
only choice, one between fall
and flight. Like this, the dog
taught me how flesh
may stretch beyond itself.
Like this, I ran and ran and
ran wherever willed the animal.

When I Reach for Your Pulse (again)

I am trying to get to the   in matter that is fluid—

       melted candlewax   new moon   AUM   Floridian gulf—
       the terrain   personalities   and air that possess matter

When I reach for your pulse

       the wind is a muted vowel
       in the brush of maples and sidewalk leaves

whose aspirated breaths roll into

       up and into my ears

When I reach for your pulse

       my mind thinks it hears
       my name   It hears traffic

squeaking on tar   When I reach

       your body thuds onto the floor

below the sheriff's blade—

I feel each pound

of your feet descending our stairs in rage
Fingers sink into the cool tissue of mother's arm

before your throat summons her away

Soundwaves shake the eardrum's cells made of Rutherfordian
atoms—ninety-nine percent   . Small bones marrow-
filled, yet ninety-nine percent   . Learn rage as
heirloom—mute vibration passed through   to the
snail, neurons chanting—*name, name, name*—rattling the
Rutherfordian brain. The mind's   escapes into
background traffic, transmutes   and particles to fear:
a gulp rising.   means to make itself heard.

When I reach for your pulse

we are in Orlando by the pigskin grace
of the Citrus Bowl where Lloyd Carr

will be hoisted off the field after knocking

       Tim Tebow off his cross   You stand

       at the Holiday Inn lobby counter

your daughter and I sitting behind you

       three-quarters of a family   momentarily

       alone as the clerk retrieves our keys

When your shorts fall to the floor

       from your too-loose belt   your grin

       spans the gap between fallen leather

       and your chin   quells the tendons in my neck

       Your desperate hands permit us laughter   grasping

       shorts before the white clerk can read *Fruit*

       of the Loom   When I reach for your pulse

I confront the lack

of moments in which we laughed   I seek

solace beyond spectating   When

I reach I am listening for the   for the Atlantic, also
ninety-nine percent   , gifted body by the spasmodic
waltz of electrons. When I reach for your   , I breathe
oxygen and hydrogen atoms displaced from another. I exhale
carbon, render it lifeless. Breathe in   . Breathe out   .
When I reach for your wrist I try not

to think of the cicada's   , its hum in my palm. I
assert   as a must. My mind is the water comprising
70% of your   . I run toward the longest wavelengths
in your   , strengthen lungs, expand thoracic
to revive the Kingfisher I imagine surviving in a displaced nest
behind your   . When I reach for your pulse I theorize
how if I repeat this touch infinitely, my fingertips, eventually,
will flap like some   through your   . When I

reach for your pulse   I retreat

        into the banyan root's crook
        where I rest when I sit

closing my eyes   where I do all I can

        to air with my nose
        in breath's subconscious tense

When I reach for your pulse   I speak to myself

        in imperatives. Hold this dark   of matter in
        your   . Feel it knock your   . The half-moon
        lights the eight-year-old child in you. The child runs to spin
        the precarious cube in Ann Arbor—the   pivoted in
        cement. Slow steps, churning legs, spinning   . When I
        reach for your pulse your   's electrons shift perpetual,
        perpetuate illusion. The body doesn't crumble for unexpected
        reason. All   fluxes,

danger without escape   When I reach
for your pulse I am sitting on your lap

as you let me drive around the cul-de-sac

You are an orbital I cannot escape   I
tethered to round a nucleus   spin

on momentum   only to slow by force

of toes of legs of skin
of arms of wrists of hands

of joints of nails   All magic

starts in the vast   between electrons
in fingertips   wands attempting   again and again

and again and again   a final trick—

Reincarnation

we'll remember each other from where you hang
from ambiguous suburban maple   at night displaced in sleepless leaves you'll fall
an unripe fig

fruit falls because of our gaze—
gravity is an angry   unseen thing

I'll be the tamarind
between your teeth—
chewed   bled sour

the flinch in your vein

Suicide Note in absentia, *Part 3*

—*In the dream, again, you slept with another man. The dream marched me eleven paces down the hall to your room where I stood over your body. My wife, lying on your bed you told me my dream was not real. Have you felt your head throttled by invisible hands? This rage: that which knows no origin;— Or forgets. I slammed the door behind me* ~~and watched you blacken your own eye with your own fist.~~ *The last time I hit you, I cannot remember . . . You knew it was worse to make me watch. You knew how to heel these dogs.*

~

—*After 31 years of service, an envelope threatens my white coat. If I tell them the truth . . . If I tell them that in my mind groans a dissonant choir would they agree to go under my knife? For 31 years, I have operated with a stable hand in my secure occupation without malpractice. For 31 years . . . I have lived hosting the larynx of a virus in my mind. You must have known;— I could read your eyes, but your patience drove and kept me alive. At home, you preoccupied our betās. They admired your patient mind. I feared unmooring. For 31 years, had you or I divulged my secret, how many cancers would have killed? Unmoored, they wonder why I lie.*

82

~

—When the bell rang, I knew it was our son.
He wanted to watch Michigan's opener with me. I knew he only
wanted to watch and cheer and he wanted to do this together;—
But new voices have been rising in my throat . . . My arms greeted
him at the car with a heap of dry cleaning. Since you left, my once
200-pound frame has grown frail. Lucid now, in the basement,
cable in palm, I understand the need for clean tailored suits . . .
Helpless, our son's dour face hung tall in the driveway, suspicious
of my hands rifling through the possessions in his car. Help, *he*
said, Help, *he told me I needed.* THIEF! *my mouth called him*
as I sunk into the passenger seat. He pleaded, Let's just watch the
game. *I cursed Bhagavan for his name, said* DRIVE. *He obeyed*
my command. Now, I have called him four times without reply,
dammit;— Ingrate. Cable in my palm . . . he will last remember
my hand grabbing the wheel, steering his car over the curb.

ॐ नमो नारायणाय

ॐ नमो नारायणाय

ॐ नमो नारायणाय

ॐ नमो नारायणाय

ॐ नमो नारायणाय

ॐ नमो नारायणाय

ॐ नमो नारायणाय

ॐ नमो नारायणाय

ॐ नमो नारायणाय

ॐ नमो नारायणाय

ॐ नमो नारायणाय

ॐ नमो नारायणाय

ॐ नमो नारायणाय

ॐ नमो नारायणाय

ॐ नमो नारायणाय

ॐ नमो नारायणाय

ॐ नमो नारायणाय

ॐ नमो नारायणाय

ॐ नमो नारायणाय

ॐ नमो नारायणाय

ॐ नमो नारायणाय

ॐ नमो नारायणाय

ॐ नमो नारायणाय

Midwest Physics: Third Law

at the Bob Evans on Harvest Lane
Bapu ordered his western omelet
no ham and I told him I was dropping
out of medical school
foreclosing on my filial debt

my country teaches   for any refusal
retaliation   on the ride home from school
after 9/11   a white man flipped us off
our evasion   *we are Hindu*

how brahmin   the slide step
how american   the elision
perhaps these laws stretch
beyond borders   undetained

Bapu's fork scraped the plate   a jay
alighted on a power line   beside a pair
of red sneakers swaying under the loop
someone tied of their laces   under the moon

in May's blue sky   I swirled pancake
in the maple's blood   Bapu tried and failed
to say   *all my hard work   for you*
to become a bum   now that he is gone

what's my equal and opposing
force?   for each omission between us
dear Father dear country   what's the word?
for every noose   someone must cut the thread

Effigy (again)

I waited
all my life
for my Bapu
to die

When he finally
died   caged
voices escaped
his skull   They
whipped through

the neighborhood
maples   each trunk
an asthmatic wheeze
into the canopy   each

branch the treble
of my arm   fallen
on his vacant
chest

Eyes scattered
among felled leaves
I touched the cold
flesh   that snapped
its own beat

When Bapu
finally died we
cut him from
the ceiling
fed him
sweets

dipped him
in oil and
burned

the stubborn body

Radial

I wake from the mare mid-night   turn onto my shoulder
and let fall the sweat of my right hand upon your sleeping wrist
fingers walk to your radial artery

love   listen   if you can in your dream hear
through air humming with what reddens your blood   listen
how you still me back to sleep

(1   2   3   4   5   . . .

your heart so large it pumps   even in your wrist
leaves your chest to yoke the collapsing dresser's wooden creak
with the spiracles of fungus gnats sleeping in our potted cyclamen

your beat coheres the windblown eucalyptus scraping the tin roof
with the dishwasher's scrubbing of plates we couldn't bring our hands
to clean   beautiful machinery   free our palms to recover

(37   38   39   40   41   . . .

other wonders—   my diaphragm aping the rhythm of your lungs   a gnat
flailing its wings in protest against my forehead   on this the eve
of its larvae's neem-poisoned death   I will not lift my palm to harm

so long as I rest my fingers here   I who too have inhaled many poisons

yet insist on perpetual breath   not unlike the gnat   limbs compelled

by the vestigial desire to feel each moment I can   how alive we are

Man of the House Falls in Obeisance to the Saint of the Otherwise Frugal

The entire universe is suspended from me as my necklace of jewels.
—Bhagavad Gita Ch. 7 V. 7 (translation by Eknath Easwaran)

      The first time home alone   I cracked the safe in Bapu's bedroom
where my mother kept her jewelry

      Ear to the turning knob   attentive as a mother cleaning her child's
lobes with a bobby pin's looped end   my malleus felt the mechanism fall into
its gap

      I basked in the exhale of a steel door swung open   inhaled what
Mom   Saint of the Otherwise Frugal   deemed precious

      She who clipped coupons for yogurt   toilet paper   and
detergent   and then frequented the jewelry stores in Indian strip malls
that speckle the outskirts of American cities

      Gold   white gold   ruby   lapis   stones whose names I didn't
know   only the tin of chains pressed to my nose   vertebral cool
their shine calling my ten-year-old self beautiful as I stood before the mirror

Pliant   I listened for my parents' return   allowing time enough to replace   exactly where I found them   the tens of jewels laced around my neck

My holy ritual   cherishing the fugitive body

Until middle school   when in the basement's blue glow   glued with friends to the scrambled channels on cable's edge   I learned the safer trappings of male desire

In that suburban sangha   I inherited the oral tradition of fathers how to funnel myriad impulses into a replicant's deadened want

Say *tap*

Say *piece*

Feign confidence

Speak low

I locked the safe   turned away from the mirror

Assimilated to the commune's compulsion   allowed my desire to
be owned

I lost myself in the barroom din of the Tigers in the bottom of the
9th   abandoned my malleable ears to the backslapping joke of manhood
the imperial prescription to confine spirits to glass

When Bapu died   Uncle told me *Be a man   be strong*

I never wept for the universes foreclosed   when a boy imagines
himself a warrior   only to collapse like Arjun on a battle's eve

Now   two decades and an ocean away from the door in which
I last secretly held those chains and stones   I walk the street a longtime
stranger to the bejeweled boy

She who taught me Krishna's words calls to share a tiny joy   a
jewelry splurge   a gold ring and a bangle

My crooked lips part   and with one half-smiled sharp exhale
through the nose I rebuke her money wasted   her *materialism*

She hangs up

Wind shapes a row of golden leaves into a necklace on the sidewalk

It glints   knowingly   into me

Dear Paranoia,

*The suicide rate for Asian-Americans (6.10 per 100,000) is about half
that of the national rate (11.5 per 100,000).
About 75 percent of those who die by suicide give warning signs.
—APA, 2012*

Gift your double helix   to the mouth
No matter how we grow   roots bind will

wind still blows   Fallacy   Spring casts shadows
below the creek's ice   Sun slips through creases

between blinds   bleeds color in garments hung to dry
through windows   We cannot predict the arbitrary

warning sign   to which shade greens will fade
This tree   strung by miscarriage's shadow   bends

stripped limbs too long in sun   Disjunction   my lip's
crook   my slow chew   He left no note

Dear inheritance   let us relent
to inevitable passing seasons   I know

you just want me to survive

Wedding

for T

paired up ducks give their partners space   it's february
frozen patches of creek   offer platforms for preening

the green sheen of one sitting glistens   his partner stands above
on sunned rock   scraping orange feet in her maw   they're two in a flock
some fishing   some caught in current like a child   in a water park and

there I go   human seeking analog   in a world withdrawn from my walk
bipedal tedium   body in wraps that moseys romantic through winter

under ravens   as if there's nowhere better to fly   no better way
to pass time   no squirrel no dog no other human

from here to the horizon   no flora no bear no
surprise flourish   just the ducks   paired up   the partner leaping

clean feet into the creek   withdrawn from the world of her mate
a nestled bowl-shaped tub on ice   I turn away   continue walking
the trail toward marriage   you off somewhere with a friend

a book a boiling pot of tea   these steps   the only work joy asks of us
to let be what we love   and keep sharp the body's blades

New Definition of Blues

after Mississippi John Hurt

Does a stone gifted movement give a damn
about anything meaning anything. Would a sparrow, tired of singing
the same song day after day bark if given the choice. Like you

these are not questions for no reason. The breeze tastes
rosemilk and the evening sounds—cars   leaves   friction
occasional passersby—smooth into and out of the same drone.

I'm all ears—a bag of tortellini filled with paneer. In the humid
air warm as curdled milk, my shoulders loosen as a dog
growls, as the sparrow stomps in a puddle

before the bird flies to peck my shells. World, have me.
As long as wings unfurl and taunt, I'll keep
scratching at the bark until I'm gone

Netī Netī

Yasmāt parataram nāsti
neti netīti vai śrutiḥ,

Nothing exists higher than That
which is described as "not this, not this,"

When I find your body

I feel no tears   No joy   No
anger   No relief   When I reach

for your carotid   it is no out of body

experience   no warbler on its last
breath   no morning mist rising

off a highway   meadow   or sound

When I find you dead   Bapu

it is everything

No sun on my soaked back in the midst

of a mountain storm   No tanpura's drone

oozing over the sitar's lick   When I reach

for your wrist   it is no samādhi

No hailmary   No defeat

Dead   you are everything

these trees   their roots   their disease

the house's foundation   pillar   and demolition

Not the rain

stinging your daughter's brow   not the strand
of hair greying at your wife's temple

not your son cold as a stethoscope

silent on a bare chest
When I reach for your pulse

my mouth holds nothing

but my name for your stubbled chin
and   no

this is not enough

it is everything

manasā vacasā caiva
nityam arādhayed gurum.

remember That always with
mind and speech

ॐ नमो नारायणाय

ॐ नमो नारायणाय

ॐ नमो नारायणाय

ॐ नमो नारायणाय

ॐ नमो नारायणाय

ॐ नमो नारायणाय

ॐ नमो नारायणाय

ॐ नमो नारायणाय

ॐ नमो नारायणाय

ॐ नमो नारायणाय

ॐ नमो नारायणाय

ॐ नमो नारायणाय

Notes

The first line of "Effigy" is borrowed from Dawn Lundy Martin's book *Discipline* (Nightboat, 2011) in which the text says "I waited all my life for my father to die and when he did I felt empty." (p. 38) This poem emerged in response.

The Midwest Physics series of poems are titled after Newton's laws of motion that frame the physical nature of reality in terms of forces enacted upon discrete objects.

Newton's First Law is a rephrasing of Galileo's Law of Inertia, stating that an object in motion (or at rest) will maintain its velocity unless acted upon by a net external force or an unbalanced force. In "Midwest Physics: First Law," Syria, Somalia, Yemen, and Afghanistan are cited from various August and September headlines throughout the 90s and early 2000s referring to US Military strikes and/or surveillance projects from the Gulf War through the post-9/11 wars, all happening in the backdrop of my football-watching suburban Ohio childhood. The Watson Institute at Brown University estimates that these US military efforts post-9/11 have displaced at least 38 million people in those countries in addition to the Philippines, Libya, and Pakistan. https://watson.brown.edu/costsofwar/costs/human

Newton's Second Law of Motion can be represented by the equation Force = Mass x Acceleration. This describes situations in which an unbalanced force acts upon an object thus changing its velocity. You can calculate the acceleration (change in velocity) by dividing the summation of forces (and their vectors) by the mass of the object.

Newton's Third Law is colloquially represented by the phrase "Every action has an equal and opposite reaction."

The end of the concluding haiku to "Funeral: Durga Puja" borrows from Roger Caillois's quotation of Pytahgoras in Caillois's 1935 essay "Mimicry and Legendary Psychasthenia."

The conception of "*Suicide Note* in absentia" is indebted to Frank Bidart's long persona poems.

"*Suicide Note* in absentia" and other poems in the manuscript include creolizations of Gujarati, Hindi, and English particular to the speakers' home life. I performed an earlier version of the first third of Part 3 of "*Suicide Note* in absentia" as a half choreographed/half improvised piece at Counterpath in Denver in March 2018.

"Attachment" quotes slokas from the "Saraswati Vandana Mantra."

The italicized lines in the penultimate stanza of "Conditional Bridges" comes from Chloe Honum's poem "Spring."

Sanskrit quotations that frame the "Morning Chant" poems and "Netī Netī" come from *The Guru Gita*. The italicized English lines below the quoted text are not translations, but responses loosely derived from translations.

The first draft of "Viveka Vairāgya at the Amtrak Station" was created through a somatic ritual in which a word emerges from the body to encapsulate "the feeling that arises in the intercostal spaces between ribs in response to grief."

"Double Slit" adapts a line from Roger Reeves' "Before Diagnosis." The double slit experiment—or in its initial incarnation, Young's Interference Experiment—was the first experiment to show that light displayed properties of both particle and wave. Future incarnations of the double slit experiment would also lead to theories of the observer effect where quantum phenomena behave differently in the presence of an observer or measurement device.

"*I Saw You and I Learned This, Beloved*" is one way to translate the title of the Hindi film song quoted in the poem "Tujhe Dekha Toh," written by Jatin Lalit and featured in the 1995 film *Dilwale Dulhania Le Jayenge*. Other italicized lines on the right margin are from the chorus of "Tujhe Dekha Toh."

The epigraph to "Love Story with Rolex" is a quote from Divya Victor in an interview with Mg Roberts published on Entropy Magazine entitled "On How and Kith: An Interview with Divya Victor." https://entropymag.org/on-how-and-kith-an-interview-with-divya-victor/
Thank you to *Entropy* magazine for permission.

"Nāranga aurantium" is the scientific name for "bitter orange" with the diacritical mark added to reflect its Indo-Dravidian root. Srinivas Kuchibhotla was murdered in Olathe, Kansas, on February 22, 2017, in a terrorist attack by a white shooter who was ex-Navy. Kuchibhotla worked as an engineer at Garmin. That same week in Sylvania, Ohio, a white woman, a patient, verbally berated my mother as she was helping schedule the woman's follow-up medical exam.

"Raga of Bapu's Hand as Brueghel's *Icarus* with Rilke and a Swami in It" adapts and morphs language from a line of Rilke's (or was it Roethke?) that I once read and have been unable to retrieve, and quotes a title of a booklet by Swami Vivekananda entitled *Thoughts of Power*.

"Scaffold" borrows and repurposes text from Lisa Robertson's essay "Doubt and the History of Scaffolding" as published in *Occasional Work and Seven Walks from the Office for Soft Architecture* (3rd Edition, Coach House Books, 2011); Gregory Kan's *This Paper Boat* (Auckland University Press, 2016); the *Yoga Vāsishta*; Solmaz Sharif's *Look* (Graywolf, 2016); and Gertrud von le Fort's 1931 novella *The Song at the Scaffold*, translated from the original German to English by Olga Marx (Ignatius Press, 2011): text is cited from pps. 98, 100, 99, 83, 45, and 100 (in order of appearance in the poem). Thank you to Ignatius Press for use of quotes from *The Song at the Scaffold*, Auckland University Press for use of quote from *This Paper Boat by* Gregory Kan, Coach House Books for use of quotes from Lisa Robertson for the epigraph to the poem "Scaffold", and American Heritage Dictionary for use of quotes for the epigraph to the poem "Scaffold".

The first draft of "Scaffold" was written in response to a walking ritual and owes a debt to Julie Carr, Gesel Mason, Janet Cardiff, Lisa Robertson, and the other sources mentioned above.

Marie de l'Incarnation in *The Song at the Scaffold* is a fictionalized rendering of the nun Françoise Geneviève Philippe who went by the name Marie de l'Incarnation and published her own account of the events of the Carmelite nuns' martyrdom during the French Terror in an 1836 book entitled *History of the Carmelite Nuns of Compiègne.*

"Postcard from Amritsar" was written in response to a visit to Jallianwala Bagh in Amritsar, Punjab, near the Wagah Border between India and Pakistan. In April 1919, British military under the command of General Dyer fired over 1,600 rounds on Indian civilians and pilgrims gathered to celebrate the spring harvest at Jallianwala Bagh. The British claimed the death toll at 379. Indian sources estimated the toll to be over 1,000. There is a well in the center of Jallianwala Bagh into which many leapt to evade bullets. One film depiction of this scene can be found in the 2006 film *Rang De Basanti* directed by Rakeysh Omprakash Mehra. The film as a whole, and the scene in particular, draws parallels between the violence of British Imperial forces and the Indian government's oppressive curtailing of freedoms today.

"Exegesis as Quarter Cento from the Wagah Border" is a 25-line cento comprised of lines from the following sources: Amiri Baraka "Beginnings: Malcolm"; 2. Aase Berg "Life Form"; 3. Nguyen Trai "Mai (Apricot)"; 4. Arvind Malhotra's translation of Kabir "KGG 1.146"; 5. Graham Foust "This Poem"; 6. Theresa Hak Kyung Cha "Dictee"; 7. Lorna Goodison "Turn Thanks to Miss Mirry"; 8. Ruth Ellen Kocher "Meditation on Breathing"; 9. Andrew Joron "Confession on Method"; 10. Sueyeun Juliette Lee "Solar Maximum"; 11. Gaston Bachelard *Poetics of Space*; 12. Nin Andrews "Dear Professor"; 13. Walter Benjamin "Baudelaire" from *The Arcades Project*; 14. Andrew Joron, "Serialism, Reconsidered"; 15. Tracy K. Smith "The Universe is a House Party"; 16. Rajiv Mohabir "Canis Latrans"; 17. Ocean Vuong "To my Father / To my Future Son"; 18. Robert Creeley "Heaven Knows"; 19. Ken Chen "Taipei Novel"; 20. Charles Baudelaire "Planning"; 21. Pablo Neruda "The Stolen Branch"; 22. Bhanu Kapil "Schizophrene"; 23. D.C. Lau's translation of Lao Tzu's *Tao te Ching*; 24. Eknath Easwaran's translation of the *Bhagavad Gita*; and 25. Wallace Stevens "Thirteen Ways of Looking at a Blackbird"

"Reincarnation": reworks an image/phrase ("sleepless leaves") from francine j. harris's poem "in."

"Man of the House Falls in Obeisance to the Saint of the Otherwise Frugal" owes a hidden debt to the Borg in various *Star Trek* series as an analogy to the assimilative pressures of gender. The epigraph is from the *Bhagavad Gita*. Translated by Eknath Easwaran. Copyright 1985, 2007 by the Blue Mountain Center of Meditation. Used with permission.

"Wedding" is in the form of a gigan, a sixteen-line form invented by Ruth Ellen Kocher that utilizes a refrain from lines 1 and 6 in 11 and 12, respectively.

"New Definition of Blues" is written in response to Mississippi John Hurt's song "Beulah Land" and owes a debt to Shari Kane who taught me how to play the fingerstyle blues.

As with most poetry and art, influences are wide-ranging, and often inseparable from the fiction of a singular authorial voice. For any unattributed echoes of others that appear in these pages, or adaptations of lines whose origins I have failed to remember, I acknowledge my debt to the choir.

Acknowledgments

Thank you—

To the editors of the following journals and presses for publishing earlier versions of many poems in this book:

32 Poems, Adroit Journal, Alaska Quarterly Review, Boulevard Magazine, Cosmonauts Avenue, Counterclock, Down in Edin Magazine (NZ), *GASHER Journal, The Georgia Review, Indiana Review, Landfall* (NZ), *The Offing, Redivider, tap Magazine, Tin House, Tinderbox Poetry Journal, Waxwing, WINDOW* by Patient Sounds Press. Thank you to the editors of the anthology *A Clear Dawn: New Asian Voices from Aotearoa New Zealand* from Auckland University Press and to the editors of *Plume Poetry 10*. The poem "Morning Chant: Scatter" was published as a broadside by the Center for Book Arts.

To my mother Dipti and my sister Neha for supporting the collective emotional work that this writing entailed. To my late father, Bapu, for trying in the ways you could. To the Purohit and Joshi families, to my Foi and cousins, and the many ancestors and relatives I haven't had the privilege to know. To the Aunties and Uncles of the South Asian community in Northwest Ohio for helping raise me. To the Romanos and McGlynns. To Chait Mann.

To the University of Colorado-Boulder, Tin House Summer Writers' Workshop, VONA Voices, the University of Michigan and the University of Otago, for the support of time, space, and funding to write and study.

To my writing teachers: Ruth Ellen Kocher, Noah Eli Gordon, Julie Carr, Marcia Douglas, Cheryl Higashida, Jeffrey Deshell, Gesel Mason, Roger Reeves, Craig Santos Perez, Stephen Rush, and Jessica Young. In particular, to Ruth Ellen who recognized this book before I did and taught me how to shape it and reshape it. To the innumerable writers who have taught me through your words, and to those whose work I've drawn on unconsciously and therefore will only recognize my debt to you after this book is in the world. To Ruth Ellen Kocher, Rajiv Mohabir, and Diana Khoi Nguyen for the generous blurbs to accompany this book.

To Whitney Kerutis, Rajiv Mohabir, Rachelle Parker, Danny Ruiz, Natalie Sharp, Phuong Vuong, Silen Charlie Wellington, El Williams III, and CL Young for offering their time, thoughts, and care to the shape of this book. To Zak Argabrite, Huia Bramley, Nilufar Karimi, Hannah Perrin King, Claire Lacey, Jessica Lawson, Yuma Uesaka, Colin Walker, and other fellow writers for conversations that contributed to this book. To Erin Armstrong, James Ashby, Jenni Ashby, Taneum Bambrick, Jordan Birnholtz, Sam Chirtel, Ansley Clark, Cris Crocker-Escribano, Rachel Cruea, James Dulin, Amy and Dan Hayes, Chloe Honum, Amanda Galvan Hunyh, Marlin Jenkins, Shari Kane, Bhanu Kapil, Preeti Kaur, Erinrose Mager, Liz McGehee, Maddie Mori, Angel Morton, Alicia Mountain, Soham Patel, Héctor Ramírez, Mike Ranellone, Thomas Ross, Anjoli Roy, Phoebe Rusch, Michael Sackllah, Lauren Schachar, Grant Schroll, Ajooni Sethi, Parth Singh, Grant Souders, Hillary Susz, Vignesh Swaminathan, Michael Swong, Sarah Thompson, Katie Vandusen, Divya Victor, Ann Wright, fellow writers from the MFA program at the University of Colorado-Boulder, poets from Craig Santos Perez's 2018 VONA Voices Residency, and poets from Roger Reeves' 2017 Tin House Writers' Workshop, Brian Buckley and the staff at Innisfree, folks at the Heiwa house, and the many others whose words, encouragements, brilliance, and conversations stay with me.

Ngā mihi nui to the artists/writers/thinkers in Aotearoa who have welcomed me, including Hana Pera Aoake, Liz Breslin, Lynley Edmeades, Jacob Edmond, Michelle Elvy, Eliana Gray, Simon Kaan, Emer Lyons, Paula Morris, Emma Neale, Nicky Page, Robyn Maree Pickens, essa may ranapiri, Ruby Solly, Chris Tse, Louise Wallace, Alison Wong, the Octagon Poetry Collective, among many others.

To Martha Rhodes, Hannah Matheson, Ryan Murphy, Sally Ball, and the whole editorial team at Four Way Books for believing in this book and bringing it to life. To Pranati Panda for providing the gorgeous cover art.

To all those I have forgotten to mention, but who have connected with me through poems, life, conversation, or passing moments. If I have failed to mention you here, please "charge it to my head and not my heart."

To Tessa Romano, always.

Rushi Vyas was born in Toledo, Ohio. He is co-author of the chapbook *Between Us, Not Half a Saint* (GASHER Press, 2021) with Rajiv Mohabir, and his poem "Morning Chant: Scatter" was republished as a broadside by the Center for Book Arts. He earned his MFA from the University of Colorado-Boulder and his BS from the University of Michigan. His poems have been published in *Adroit Journal, The Georgia Review, Indiana Review, Landfall (NZ), The Offing, The Spinoff (NZ), Tin House,* and elsewhere. He has worked as a career counselor, curriculum developer, editor, and facilitator. In 2019, Rushi moved from Brooklyn, New York, to Ōtepoti Dunedin, Aotearoa New Zealand, where he currently lives, writes, and teaches.

Publication of this book was made possible by grants and donations. We are also grateful to those individuals who participated in our Build a Book Program. They are:

Anonymous (13), Robert Abrams, Michael Ansara, Kathy Aponick, Jean Ball, Sally Ball, Clayre Benzadón, Adrian Blevins, Laurel Blossom, adam bohannon, Betsy Bonner, Patricia Bottomley, Lee Briccetti, Joel Brouwer, Susan Buttenwieser, Anthony Cappo, Paul and Brandy Carlson, Mark Conway, Elinor Cramer, Dan and Karen Clarke, Kwame Dawes, Michael Anna de Armas, John Del Peschio, Brian Komei Dempster, Rosalynde Vas Dias, Patrick Donnelly, Lynn Emanuel, Blas Falconer, Jennifer Franklin, John Gallaher, Reginald Gibbons, Rebecca Kaiser Gibson, Dorothy Tapper Goldman, Julia Guez, Naomi Guttman and Jonathan Mead, Forrest Hamer, Luke Hankins, Yona Harvey, KT Herr, Karen Hildebrand, Carlie Hoffman, Glenna Horton, Thomas and Autumn Howard, Catherine Hoyser, Elizabeth Jackson, Linda Susan Jackson, Jessica Jacobs and Nickole Brown, Lee Jenkins, Elizabeth Kanell, Nancy Kassell, Maeve Kinkead, Victoria Korth, Brett Lauer and Gretchen Scott, Howard Levy, Owen Lewis and Susan Ennis, Margaree Little, Sara London and Dean Albarelli, Tariq Luthun, Myra Malkin, Louise Mathias, Victoria McCoy, Lupe Mendez, Michael and Nancy Murphy, Kimberly Nunes, Susan Okie and Walter Weiss, Cathy McArthur Palermo, Veronica Patterson, Jill Pearlman, Marcia and Chris Pelletiere, Sam Perkins, Susan Peters and Morgan Driscoll, Maya Pindyck, Megan Pinto, Kevin Prufer, Martha Rhodes, Paula Rhodes, Louise Riemer, Peter and Jill Schireson, Rob Schlegel, Yoana Setzer, Soraya Shalforoosh, Mary Slechta, Diane Souvaine, Barbara Spark, Catherine Stearns, Jacob Strautmann, Yerra Sugarman, Arthur Sze and Carol Moldaw, Marjorie and Lew Tesser, Dorothy Thomas, Rushi Vyas, Martha Webster and Robert Fuentes, Rachel Weintraub and Allston James, Abigail Wender, D. Wolff, and Monica Youn.